Ripley's
Believe It or Not!®

Developed and produced by Ripley Publishing Ltd

This edition published and distributed by:

Mason Crest
450 Parkway Drive, Suite D, Broomall, PA 19008
www.masoncrest.com

Printed and bound in the United States of America

9 8 7 6 5 4 3 2

Ripley's Believe It or Not!
Curious Critters
ISBN: 978-1-4222-3141-8 (hardback)
Ripley's Believe It or Not!—Complete 8 Title Series
ISBN: 978-1-4222-3138-8

Cataloging-in-Publication Data is on file with the Library of Congress

PUBLISHER'S NOTE
While every effort has been made to verify the accuracy of the entries in this book, the
Publishers cannot be held responsible for any errors contained in the work. They would
be glad to receive any information from readers.

WARNING
Some of the stunts and activities in this book are undertaken by experts and should not
be attempted by anyone without adequate training and supervision.

Ripley's Believe It or Not!

Dare To Look

CURIOUS CRITTERS

www.MasonCrest.com

CURIOUS CRITTERS

Awesome animals. Look inside and be amazed by some extraordinary animals. Meet the jet-skiing dog, the incredible shark whisperer, and the snowboarding opossum!

Kyndra Batia of Garden City, Texas, sent
Ripley's this amazing picture of a baby
goat with just one eye...

CATCOPTER

▶ After his pet tabby cat was killed by a car, Dutch artist Bart Jansen turned the animal's body into a radio-controlled flying model helicopter. Bart kept Orville (named after aviation pioneer Orville Wright) in a freezer for six months before having him stuffed. He then attached propellers to each of the cat's paws and an engine inside his stomach to create the "Orvillecopter," a "half cat, half machine" that can fly at a considerable speed. A fin attached to Orville's tail aids steering. He has also been fitted with a plastic undercarriage to allow dignified landings.

CAT FLAP

▶ Having driven around for hours mystified as to why his car was struggling for power, a motorist in Rio Verde, Brazil, checked under the hood—and found a kitten stuck inside the engine. It was trapped inside the metal air intake pipe, with just its head and a paw sticking out. Firefighters used a hacksaw to cut the kitten free and, incredibly, it survived. It had climbed into the engine to keep warm but had then been suddenly sucked in when the driver started up the car.

MISSING PET▶ Monika Moser of Munich, Germany, was reunited with her pet cat Poldi more than 16 years after he went missing. He walked out of the family home in 1996 and was not seen again until he was found 20 mi (32 km) away living in a forest and was identified by a mark on his ear.

MASTER MIMIC ▶ Chook, a superb lyrebird at Australia's Adelaide Zoo, learned to mimic perfectly the sounds of construction, including drills, handsaws, trucks, and radio conversations, while workers were near his enclosure.

TV STAR ▶ Seeking a warm refuge from an unseasonal blizzard, Laura the cow escaped from her field in Serfaus, Austria, and walked into a sportswear store at a nearby shopping mall, chewing her way through two bras and a T-shirt. The sports company, Intersport, was so impressed by Laura's taste that it signed her up as the star of its new TV advertising campaign.

HAMSTER RAMPAGE ▶ Houdini the hamster left his owners with a £1,000 ($1,500) repair bill after escaping from his cardboard box, climbing into the car engine, and chewing through the electrics while being driven to his new home in Derbyshire, England. He was rescued from the engine after a two-hour search.

LOYAL FRIEND ▶ After 68-year-old Lao Pan, a resident of Panjiatun, China, died in November 2011, his dog took up residence by his grave site, refusing to leave even to look for food. Villagers were so touched by the dog's devotion that they brought him food and built him a graveside kennel.

BEAR BASH ▶ When a black bear tried to snatch her pet dachshund Fudge, Brooke Collins, a hairdresser from Juneau, Alaska, scared off the predator by punching it on the nose. The bear immediately let go of the dog, who escaped with minor claw and bite marks.

HUNTING LESSONS ▶ Fishermen in Honduras have been training sharks to hunt poisonous lionfish, which have invaded a reef near the island of Roatan and whose voracious appetite is reducing local fish stocks and threatening the fishermen's livelihood. Sharks had always avoided lionfish because of their spikes, but when fishermen started spearing the lionfish and leaving them alive and struggling in the sea, they found that the sharks soon became attracted to them and learned to recognize them as natural prey.

TRAIN JOURNEY ▶ A lucky black cat survived a 120-mi (193-km) rail journey from Southampton, England, to Cardiff, Wales, in June 2012 by clinging on to the underside of the train.

FUGITIVE PENGUIN ▶ A Humboldt penguin that jumped over a wall and slipped through a fence at the Tokyo Sea Life Park remained on the loose for 82 days in the Japanese capital before finally being caught. While on the run, the penguin was frequently spotted swimming in rivers but always managed to elude keepers.

KITTEN RESCUE ▶ A mother cat and her three kittens were rescued from beneath the concrete floor of a garage in a house in West Jordan, Utah. They had crept into the space beneath the floor shortly before the concrete was poured, but when construction workers heard meowing, they cut a hole in the newly laid floor so that the animals could be saved.

RAISED ALARM ▶ When disabled Victoria Shaw of Wrexham, North Wales, collapsed in the shower, Louis, her Yorkshire terrier, summoned help by pressing the panic alarm in her home. She had trained him to hit the button in case of an emergency, and was delighted when he remembered what to do.

EASY RIDER

▶ Tom Bennett and his dog Brody, a five-year-old golden doodle, ride on a jet ski on Pigeon Lake near Bobcaygeon in Ontario, Canada. Brody, who has only ever fallen off once, wears goggles to keep dragonflies from hitting him in the eyes.

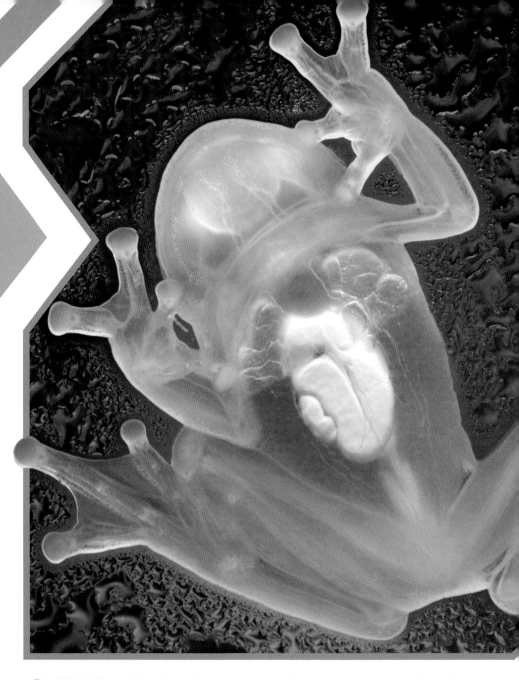

MIGHTY MICE▶ Birds nesting on Gough Island in the South Atlantic Ocean risk being eaten by packs of the 700,000 oversized mice that populate the island. The mice have evolved into super-rodents that are three times the size of the normal house mouse. Instead of being vegetarian, these monster mice have turned into carnivores that eat chicks from their nests.

BAT INVASION▶ The town of Katherine in Australia's Northern Territory was invaded by more than 250,000 fruit bats in February 2012. The risk of catching rabies from a bat bite or scratch was sufficient for authorities to close down the town's main sports ground until the bats left.

THICK COAT▶ The sea otter has the thickest coat of any mammal, with a million hairs covering an area the size of a postage stamp.

QUICK CHANGE▶ As the species consists largely of males, the two-banded anemonefish, a native of the Red Sea, has males that can turn into female fish at will, in order to mate.

SEE-THROUGH FROG

▶ *Glass frogs from the forests of Central and South America have a transparent skin through which you can see their beating heart, and their stomach, liver, intestines, lungs, and gall bladder. Their green translucent body enables them to blend in with their leafy background, thereby protecting them from predators.*

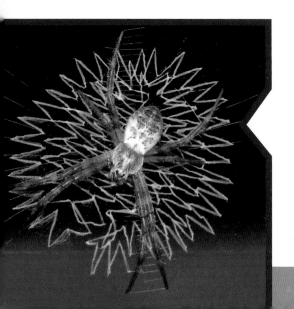

BLOOD SUCKER▶ The Cooper's nutmeg snail searches the sea floor in the Eastern Pacific Ocean for electric rays. It then climbs on top of them and drinks their blood.

GEOMETRIC WEB

▶ An orb-weaver spider in a Hong Kong park spun this incredible web in an intricate geometric shape. These amazing patterns are believed to attract insect prey by reflecting ultraviolet light. They may also help camouflage the spider from predators.

LUNCH LAUNCH▶ To catch seals off the coast of Cape Town, South Africa, 2,000-lb (900-kg) sharks swim up rapidly from beneath, sometimes launching both themselves and their prey as high as 10 ft (3 m) out of the water.

ETERNAL YOUTH▶ Honey bees can reverse the brain decline brought on through old age by tackling duties usually done by much younger bees. Scientists at Arizona State University found that when older, foraging bees were tricked into doing social tasks inside the nest, the molecular structure of their brain changed, significantly improving their ability to learn new things.

CANNIBAL TOADS▶ As much as 66 percent of a young Australian cane toad's diet is made up of other, smaller cane toads.

STOWAWAY LIZARD▶ A stowaway 6-in-long (15-cm) brown *Chioninia* lizard not only survived a 3,000-mi (4,800-km) flight in passenger Sue Banwell-Moore's luggage as she returned from vacation in the Cape Verde Islands to the U.K., it also coped with her inadvertently putting it into the washing machine along with her dirty laundry. She spotted the lizard as she was hanging out the washing after 30 minutes on the delicates cycle. Nicknamed Larry, the lizard recovered from its ordeal and now lives at a nearby wildlife park.

ANT RAFTS▶ Fire ants can survive flood conditions for weeks at a time by linking together to form living rafts with their bodies. Their hairy bodies allow the ants to trap air bubbles, which, with all the insects jammed together, fuse to form a protective air layer that stops the colony from drowning. A single raft can contain more than 10,000 ants.

MIRROR TRICK▶ To encourage its lonely flamingos to breed, China's Shenzhen Zoo surrounded their enclosure with 45 ft (14 m) of mirrors, each over 3 ft (90 cm) high, to make them feel as if they were in a large colony. When the birds first arrived at the zoo from Japan, they failed to breed because their flock was too small for them to feel confident enough to have chicks.

CORPSE CARRIER
▶ To deter predators such as spiders, the assassin bug of Malaysia makes itself look bigger by carrying at least 20 dead ants on its back at a time. The assassin bug kills the ants by injecting them with a deadly saliva containing an enzyme that quickly turns their insides to liquid. The liquid lunch is then sucked up by the bug and the dry carcasses are heaped on its back.

GIANT WASP▶ A newly discovered giant wasp on the island of Sulawesi, Indonesia, is 2½ in (6.4 cm) long and has jaws longer than its front legs.

WING SONG▶ The club-winged manakin, which lives in the forests of Colombia and Ecuador, is the only bird known to sing with its wings. Whereas most birds have lightweight, hollow wing bones, the club-winged manakin has dense, solid wing bones that help it to emit a violin-like sound. To attract a mate, instead of singing through its beak, it rubs its wings together.

DESIGNER SHEEP▶ The latest collectible for wealthy Chinese people is a $2-million Dolan sheep bred in the ancient city of Kashgar. With their distinctive curved nose, twin tail, and floppy ears, there are only 1,000 Dolan sheep in the world.

TAKE ME HOME▶ A lost budgerigar was taken back to its home after reciting its entire address to a police officer. The talkative bird had escaped from a house in Yokohama, Japan, and flown to a city center hotel where it was caught and handed over to the police.

SELF-SUFFICIENT▶ Yeti crabs grow their own food. The crabs, which are found near deep hydrothermal vents, get most of their food from bacteria that they cultivate on their hairy arms.

WRONG TURN▶ In June 2011, a young emperor penguin took a wrong turn and washed ashore on a beach in New Zealand, more than 2,000 mi (3,200 km) from its Antarctic home. It was the first confirmed sighting of an emperor penguin in New Zealand for 44 years.

ALBINO TURTLE

▶*A rare albino baby green sea turtle swims at a conservation center on Khram Island, Thailand, where 15,000 turtles are hatched each year under the protection of the Thai Navy before being released into the sea.*

POPULATION PLUNGE ▶ White-rumped vultures of southern Asia once numbered in the tens of millions, but during the past ten years, the population has dropped by about 99.9 percent.

WONDER WHISKERS ▶ Dormice can climb trees by using their whiskers. The tiny animals, which spend winter on the ground but live in trees in summer, vibrate their whiskers up to 25 times a second to help them navigate their way safely along uneven branches and through tight gaps.

HIGH SPOT ▶ A cat climbed to the top of a 30-ft (9-m) saguaro cactus in the Arizona desert and stayed there for more than three days. After being filmed by a TV crew from a helicopter, the daredevil cat calmly climbed down from its lofty perch and wandered off.

HOMESICK HOUND ▶ Buck, a three-year-old Labrador, traveled 500 mi (800 km) to be reunited with his owner. No longer able to keep a dog in his Myrtle Beach, South Carolina, home, Mark Wessells had left Buck with his father in Winchester, Virginia, but the dog had other ideas and several months later turned up near his old home.

SNAKE BITE ▶ A 13-month-old toddler from Shefa'Amr, Israel, chewed the head off a snake. Little Imad Aleeyan used his six teeth to bite into the head of the 12-in-long (30-cm) nonvenomous snake.

DOG WIGS ▶ Ruth Regina from Bay Harbor Islands, Florida, makes custom wigs for dogs. Her enterprise started when her niece asked her to make a wig for her basset hound and now she sells doggie hairpieces in a wide range of styles, including the Sarah Palin, the Elvis, and the Beatle.

SECRET EATER ▶ Although giant pandas were thought to be strictly vegetarian, with 99 percent of their diet being bamboo, a camera at the Wanglong Nature Reserve in Sichuan, China, recorded on video one animal eating a dead antelope in December 2011. However, it is not thought that the panda killed the antelope, but that it stumbled across the corpse in the forest.

IMMORTAL WORMS ▶ Flatworms can regenerate time and time again, giving them the ability to live forever unless they succumb to disease or a predator. If a flatworm is cut in half, the head portion grows a tail and the tail portion grows a head—a feat that allowed scientists at Nottingham University in England to create a colony of 20,000 identical flatworms, all from one original specimen.

HIGH TEA ▶ Sure-footed Tamri goats of Morocco love the tasty berries of the argan tree so much that as many as 16 goats have been seen perched on the narrow branches of a single tree, some as high as 30 ft (9 m) above the ground. Amazingly, the goats' cloven hooves help them to climb and balance while their soft soles enable them to grip the bark of the tree.

DOUBLE TROUBLE
▶ This two-headed California Kingsnake at San Diego Zoo presents a headache for keepers at feeding time. They have to feed each head separately (covering one with a hood) in case one head tries to snatch the other's food and causes injury. The snake started out as twins, but the embryo failed to split properly, causing the rare two-headed reptile.

FOUR BEARS ▶ A bear and three cubs broke into a cabin in northern Norway and finished off all the food and drink—including marshmallows, chocolate spread, honey, and over 100 cans of beer.

KNOTTED BOAS ▶ Some captive boa constrictors and pythons suffer from a fatal disease called Inclusion Body Disease, which can cause them to tie their body in knots from which they are unable to escape. The disease is thought to be caused by a previously unknown strain of arenavirus—a type of virus that normally attacks rodents.

BLOOD LUST ▶ Some species of mosquito fly up to 40 mi (64 km) to find a meal of blood, and people can attract mosquitoes from that far away simply by breathing. When a person exhales, their carbon dioxide and other odors waft through the air, letting mosquitoes know that a tasty meal is within their flight range.

FALSE LEGS ▶ Lemon Pie, a dog from Mexico City who lost both his front legs, has learned to walk again thanks to a pair of $6,000 state-of-the-art prosthetic limbs.

GLASS WINGS

▶ The glasswing butterfly, *Greta oto*, of Central America has translucent wings that appear to be made of glass. The tissue between the veins of its wings lacks the colored scales present in other butterflies, resulting in its unique appearance and Spanish name *espejitos*, meaning "little mirrors." Although fragile-looking, the wings are just as strong as those of other butterflies and if it were not for the wings' dark orange borders, the glasswing would be virtually invisible to the human eye.

Ripley's
Believe It or Not!®
www.ripleybooks.com

◀NO NOSE

▶ *Kabang, a German shepherd cross, lost her snout while saving the lives of two young girls in a motorcycle crash in the Philippines. Her owner's daughter and niece were about to be run over by the bike until Kabang heroically stepped into its path, but in doing so the dog got her head caught in the bike's front wheel and her snout and upper jaw were ripped off. However, an Internet campaign spearheaded by Karen Kenngott, a nurse from Buffalo, New York, raised $20,000 for Kabang to be taken to the United States for remedial surgery.*

LONG TONGUE▶ First discovered in Ecuador in 2005, the tube-lipped nectar bat—*Anoura fistulata*—has a tongue that is nearly twice the length of its body. The bat is about 2 in (5 cm) long, but its tongue is nearly 3½ in (9 cm) long, giving it the longest tongue, relative to body length, of any known mammal. When not collecting nectar from flowers, the bat's tongue is retracted and stored in the animal's rib cage.

OLD TOWN▶ The world's oldest horse and the world's oldest dog both live in the same town in Essex, England. Shayne the horse is 51 years old and has lived in a Brentwood horse sanctuary since 2007 while Pip, a 24-year-old terrier-whippet cross, lives nearby with her owner Tiffany Dyer and is still active enough to perform with the Essex Dog Display Team. In human years, Pip would now be 170 years old.

INSECT LIGHTS▶ The Jamaican click beetle, the world's brightest glowing insect, was once used by tribesmen around the Caribbean to light their huts at night. Unlike other bioluminescent creatures, different Jamaican click beetles can emit different colors, ranging from green to orange.

BOOM TIME▶ Around 100 male crocodiles at a breeding farm in the Golan Heights in the Middle East began their mating calls prematurely after the animals mistook the sonic booms made by Israeli warplanes flying overhead for the calls of rival males.

ACIDIC VENOM ▶ The venom of the Texas coral snake contains compounds that produce an intense pain by making nerves react as if they are being attacked with acid.

DONKEY TRIM ▶ In June 2012, a pack of long-haired Baudet du Poitou donkeys at a farm in Hampshire, England, had their locks cut for the first time in 17 years to help them cope with the hot weather. The rare French donkeys are not normally groomed—their fur is usually left to grow into dreadlocks that stretch all the way down to the ground.

ROAR ENERGY ▶ On a still night, a lion's roar can be heard 5 mi (8 km) away. Both males and females roar, the sound starting as a low moan and progressing in stages to higher and louder tones. The roar can reach 114 decibels—louder than a jackhammer.

LARGEST EGGS ▶ Whale sharks are born from the world's largest eggs—12 in (30 cm) long—that remain in the mother's body until after the eggs hatch.

FLYING PLANKTON ▶ Tiny shrimplike plankton called copepods escape predatory fish by bursting through the surface of the ocean and flying through the air. The creatures, which live close to the surface, are so adept at this evasive action they actually travel farther in the air than in water.

DOG IN DISGUISE
▶ When they saw this strange creature roaming the streets, residents of Xinxiang, China, thought a genetically modified pig was on the run from nearby medical laboratories. In fact the animal was not a pig at all but a rare pedigree Chinese crested hairless dog whose bizarre tufty head and bare, pink, spotted body make it look much more like a pig than a dog.

INSTANT ANTLERS ▶ The blackbuck antelope, which is native to India, grows a full set of 30-in (75-cm) antlers in just 12 weeks—this is the fastest-growing body part in the animal world.

LIVING POOP ▶ After being eaten, some marine snails survive inside ducks' guts for up to five hours, even traveling many miles in flight before popping out alive and completely unscathed in the bird's feces.

WOOFSTOCK FESTIVAL ▶ More than 300,000 dog lovers and their pets attend the annual Woofstock Festival in Toronto, Canada. First held in 2003, the event includes a fashion show and a talent contest for dogs, with an award for the best-dressed dog. Yorkshire terrier Remy, dressed as a biker in a black leather jacket, helmet, and sunglasses, was the star of the 2012 show. Previous winners include a dog dressed as Bob Marley and another wearing a costume inspired by the *Men in Black* movie trilogy.

MINI LIZARD ▶ *Brookesia micra*, a newly discovered chameleon from Madagascar, reaches a maximum length of just 1.1 in (29 mm). It is the tiniest chameleon ever found and is so small it can stand on the head of a match.

VANISHING ACT ▶ The 8½-in-long (22-cm) smalleye pygmy shark of the Western Pacific Ocean has bioluminescent cells in its belly, which causes its silhouette to vanish when seen by predators from below.

BUSY BURROWERS ▶ Naked mole rats are only a few inches long, but a colony of several dozen can create an underground burrow that spans up to 20 football fields in area.

HARD TO SWALLOW
▶ This 2-ft-long (60-cm) night adder looked to have bitten off more than it could chew as it attempted to devour a toad head-first in a garden in Natal, South Africa. In a bid to swallow the toad, the snake stretched its mouth to an angle of almost 180 degrees.

ANT BRIDGE

▶ *Faced with a gap between two leaves that was several times wider than their body length, these weaver ants in Jakarta, Indonesia, showed incredible ingenuity by linking their bodies together to form a bridge that other ants in the army could then walk across.*

KILLER CROC▶
A 14½-ft-long (4.4-m) saltwater crocodile in the north of Australia ate up to nine pet dogs in a savage killing spree. The croc, which had also snatched wallabies, was eventually caught near the settlement of Daly River, 140 mi (225 km) south of Darwin.

DELAYED BIRTHS▶ An eastern diamond-back rattlesnake recently gave birth to 19 healthy offspring—10 females and nine males—five whole years after mating. The normal gestation period for rattlesnakes is six to seven months. The snake had mated in the wild as a sexually immature juvenile and had somehow managed to store the sperm in its body for five years.

LAST TORTOISE▶ For more than 40 years—up until his death in 2012—Lonesome George was the world's only remaining Pinta Island giant tortoise. Researchers had tried in vain to get him to mate, offering $10,000 to anyone who discovered a female Pinta Island giant tortoise.

RAT TRAP▶ Along with humans, the African crested rat is the only mammal that uses poison that it didn't produce itself. The rat chews the poisonous roots and bark of the acokanthera tree—the same deadly venom used to tip poison arrows—then smears the toxic slobber on its specially adapted fur to deter predators.

REVENGE MISSION▶ After being bitten by a common cobra while working in a paddy field near Kathmandu, Nepal, Mohamed Salmo Miya was so angry that he chased the snake, caught it, and bit it until he killed it.

BACK FROM THE DEAD▶ Rhino the hamster came back from the dead after clawing his way out of a 2-ft-deep (60-cm) grave. After finding the pet "cold and lifeless" in his cage, Dave Eyley of Oxfordshire, England, buried him in the garden, but the next day Rhino was seen scampering around, having dug a 2-in-wide (5-cm) hole and climbed to the surface.

▶▶ THE GIANT PANDA HAS A MORE POWERFUL BITE THAN ITS MUCH LARGER COUSIN, THE POLAR BEAR. ◀

ARTIFICIAL JELLYFISH▶ Biophysicists at Harvard University, Cambridge, Massachusetts, have built an artificial jellyfish using muscle cells from the heart of a rat, and silicone. When placed in an electric field, the synthetic creature looks, moves, and swims like a real jellyfish—but genetically it is still a rat.

KOALA CALL▶ Although koalas weigh only about 15 lb (6.8 kg), their bellow is as loud as a cow weighing more than a ton. The marsupials are able to make such loud noises to attract partners during the mating season because they have human-type voice boxes where the larynx sits deeper in the throat than it does in other species.

TINY FROG▶ A tiny frog, *Paedophryne amauensis*, has been discovered in Papua New Guinea that measures just 0.3 in (7.7 mm) in length as an adult and is so small it fits easily on a U.S. dime.

FAT CAT▶ After being kidnapped from the garden of a house in Landskron, Austria, Cupid, a 28-lb (13-kg) pedigree Maine Coon cat worth $4,500, was returned two weeks later because the thieves could not cope with the animal's enormous appetite of more than three cans of cat food at a single sitting.

SAFETY IN NUMBERS▶ Periodical cicadas are incapable of defending themselves, so the insects all emerge from the ground as adults at the same time—in their thousands—making it impossible for all of them to be eaten by predators.

LONG NERVE▶ Giraffes have a nerve that travels all the way down their neck to their chest and back up to connect the brain to their larynx—an organ that lies only inches away.

LOVE SONGS▶ Staff at Drusillas Zoo Park, Sussex, England, tried to get their Chilean flamingos in the mood for love by piping Barry White songs into their enclosure at night—and it resulted in the hatching of the zoo's first chick in three years.

WING SCENE ▶ *Macrocilix maia*, a Malaysian moth, mimics an entire scene on its wings—a pair of flies approaching bird droppings. The moth also emits a foul odor, and so tries to fool predators by both sight and smell.

ROUNDUP RABBIT ▶ Champis, a five-year-old pet dwarf rabbit owned by Nils-Erik and Greta Vigren of Käl, Sweden, rounds up and herds the farm's sheep as if he were a sheepdog. The rabbit has never been trained for the job but seems to have picked up the necessary skills from watching the actual sheepdogs on the farm.

MIGHTY BITE ▶ Scientists from Florida have found that extinct crocodiles generated bite forces in excess of 23,000 lb (10,500 kg)—that's twice as powerful as the bite of a Tyrannosaurus rex.

RELATED COWS ▶ By extracting DNA from ancient cow bones found at an Iranian archeological site, scientists have found that all the domesticated cows in the world today—that's about 1.3 billion of them—come from a herd of just 80 that existed 10,500 years ago.

ARTISTIC ELEPHANT ▶ By holding a paintbrush with her trunk, Shanti, an Indian elephant at Prague Zoo, Czech Republic, creates paintings that sell for more than $2,000 each. The proceeds from her artwork bought a new enclosure for Shanti and her herd.

CARING CAT ▶ A cat in Qingdao, China, lives in a birdcage with five chicks she has adopted. The unusual relationship began when owner Li Tongfa left the door of the birdcage open and the cat climbed in, but instead of eating the birds, she played with them.

BIRDS OF A FEATHER

▶ The normal-looking budgerigar on the left seems puzzled as to why her six-month-old offspring resembles a feather duster. The bizarre budgie from Zhengzhou, China, has long curly feathers all over its body, probably as a result of a rare mutation that causes unrestricted feather growth and leads to a decidedly disheveled appearance.

WORKING TOGETHER ▶ Elephants possess human-like powers of empathy that enable them to work together. In the wild, elephants have been seen stopping and teaming up to rescue another elephant that had fallen into a pit.

COLOR SENSITIVE ▶ Gunnison's prairie dogs, squirrel-like rodents native to the United States, can distinguish between the different colors of clothing people wear. The rodents make different alarm calls depending on whether they see a blue, a yellow, or a green shirt.

SIZZLING PORK ▶ Fifty-three pigs were electrocuted by a single lightning bolt that struck their sty in Guangming Xinqulou, China, on July 5, 2012. Farmer Mrs. Chen found them all lying on their backs, motionless, apart from one pig in the sty, which survived with a broken leg.

PIG HANGED ▶ In 1386, a pig went on trial in the French town of Falaise accused of causing the death of a child. Dressed in human clothes for the proceedings, the pig was found guilty, mutilated, and publicly hanged.

GREEN BOTTLE
BUBBLES

▶ *Martin Amm from Kronach, Germany, captured this amazing image of a green bottle fly in a meadow on a foggy morning. The bizarre-looking bubbles are actually morning dew. Martin told Ripley's that he can sometimes search for hours before he finds an insect to photograph, and that this type of super-close-up image, which requires a special lens, is easier to take on a cold morning because the cold-blooded insects can't fly away!*

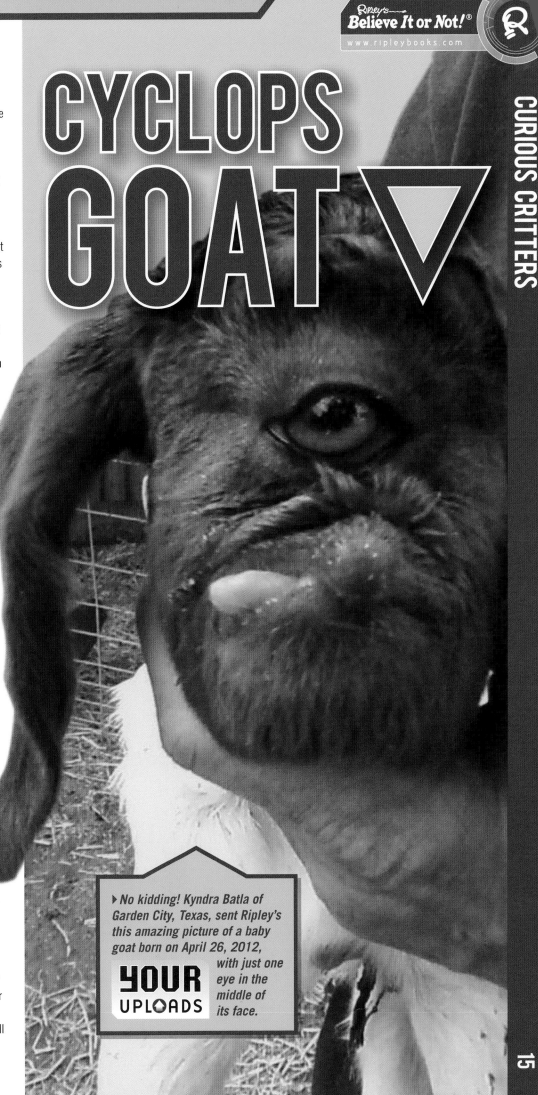

LATE DEVELOPERS▶ Female loggerhead sea turtles take as long as 45 years to mature and begin laying eggs—yet in the wild they rarely live much beyond the age of 50.

COMPLEX DNA▶ The marbled lungfish, *Protopterus aethiopicus*, has a DNA genome that is 133 base pairs long—that's 44 times longer than a human's.

DIVE BOMBING▶ Peregrine falcons can dive at over 200 mph (320 km/h), knocking smaller birds to the ground for an easy meal.

LARVAL SPRAY▶ Sweden's elk botflies spray their young into the noses of elk, where they feed on blood and mucus. Occasionally the botflies mistakenly spray a human's eyes instead. Human victims have had more than 30 eggs shot into their eye at a time. The larvae cause a burning sensation and, if not removed, attach themselves to the cornea and eyelid where they may cause extensive damage.

FEARSOME FLEAS▶ 165 million years ago, dinosaurs were plagued by giant flea-like insects—ten times the size of a modern flea—which fed on their blood with a bite thought to be as painful as being injected with a hypodermic needle.

TREE LOBSTER▶ The Lord Howe Island stick insect, aka the Tree Lobster, was rediscovered in the 21st century after being thought extinct since 1920. The size of a human hand, the insect feeds on only one species of shrub. It is thought that there are just 30 specimens in the wild—on a rat-free volcanic outcrop off the coast of Australia.

SWALLOWED SPOON▶ Fruit-loving Max, a ten-year-old Rottweiller owned by Annette Robertshaw of West Yorkshire, England, needed surgery after gulping down a strawberry... along with the teaspoon on which it was served. The spoon lodged in Max's stomach, and although it was successfully removed, the experience seems to have put him off eating strawberries for life.

GRIZZLY CUSTOMER▶ A 250-lb (113-kg), 18-month-old grizzly bear named Billy has become a regular at a pub in Vancouver, British Columbia, where he enjoys a game of pool. After going to the pub with his owners, animal handler Mark Dumas and his wife Dawn, Billy goes back to their home to watch TV, or splash and play ball with them in their swimming pool.

CYCLOPS GOAT ▽

▶ **No kidding! Kyndra Batla of Garden City, Texas, sent Ripley's this amazing picture of a baby goat born on April 26, 2012, with just one eye in the middle of its face.**

YOUR UPLOADS

Ripley's
Believe It or Not!®
www.ripleybooks.com

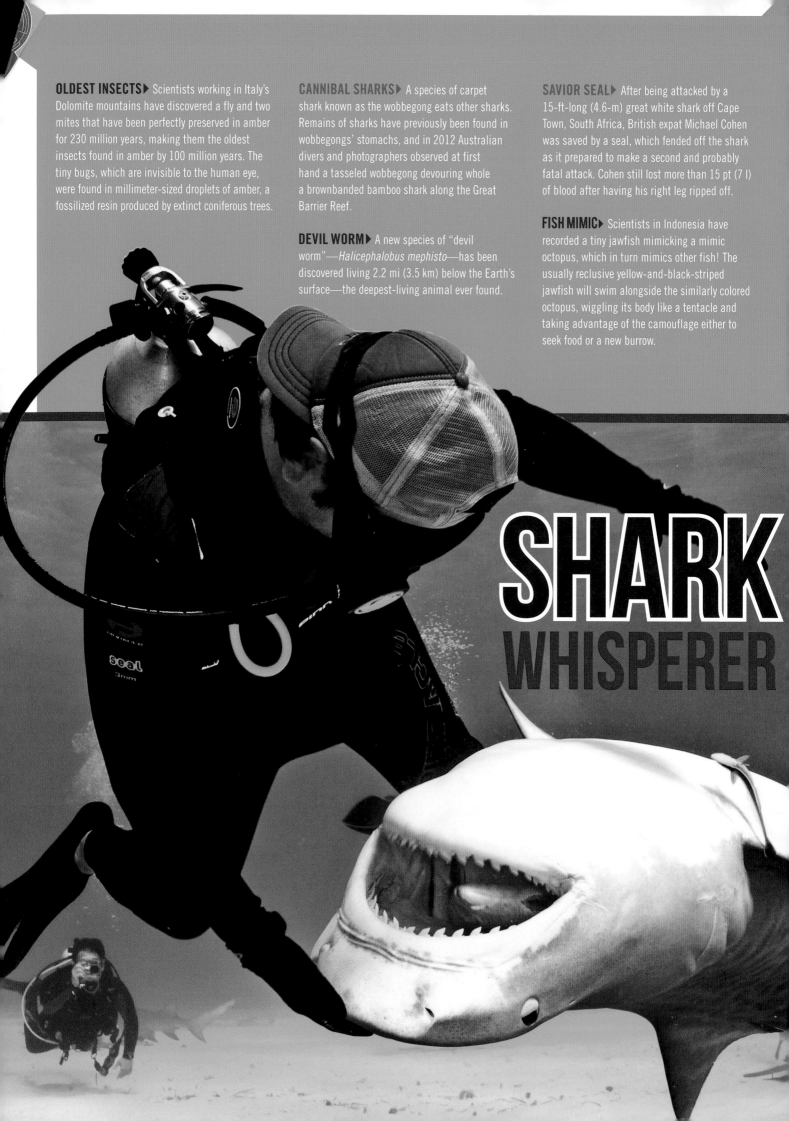

OLDEST INSECTS▶ Scientists working in Italy's Dolomite mountains have discovered a fly and two mites that have been perfectly preserved in amber for 230 million years, making them the oldest insects found in amber by 100 million years. The tiny bugs, which are invisible to the human eye, were found in millimeter-sized droplets of amber, a fossilized resin produced by extinct coniferous trees.

CANNIBAL SHARKS▶ A species of carpet shark known as the wobbegong eats other sharks. Remains of sharks have previously been found in wobbegongs' stomachs, and in 2012 Australian divers and photographers observed at first hand a tasseled wobbegong devouring whole a brownbanded bamboo shark along the Great Barrier Reef.

DEVIL WORM▶ A new species of "devil worm"—*Halicephalobus mephisto*—has been discovered living 2.2 mi (3.5 km) below the Earth's surface—the deepest-living animal ever found.

SAVIOR SEAL▶ After being attacked by a 15-ft-long (4.6-m) great white shark off Cape Town, South Africa, British expat Michael Cohen was saved by a seal, which fended off the shark as it prepared to make a second and probably fatal attack. Cohen still lost more than 15 pt (7 l) of blood after having his right leg ripped off.

FISH MIMIC▶ Scientists in Indonesia have recorded a tiny jawfish mimicking a mimic octopus, which in turn mimics other fish! The usually reclusive yellow-and-black-striped jawfish will swim alongside the similarly colored octopus, wiggling its body like a tentacle and taking advantage of the camouflage either to seek food or a new burrow.

SHARK
WHISPERER

Animal Whisperers

▶**HORSE** American horse trainer Monty Roberts believes that horses use a nonverbal language, which he calls Equus. He uses this language—a series of silent gestures—to communicate with them.

▶**LION** Using endless patience, Kevin Richardson, a ranger at the Lion Park near Johannesburg, South Africa, has developed such a rapport with lions that he has slept next to them, eaten with them, and lived with them.

▶**SNAKE** Paul Kenyon uses his experience at recognizing what mood a snake is in to catch and handle the world's most venomous snakes around his base in Western Australia.

▶**GATOR** Jeanette Rivera from the Florida's Everglades Alligator Farm, plays with and wrestles monster gators that weigh 56 lb (25 kg) more than her. She shows her confidence by placing her chin on their snout.

CONTACT LENS▶ Win Thida, a 45-year-old Asian elephant at Artis Zoo in Amsterdam in the Netherlands, was fitted with a contact lens after her eye became scratched in a fight with another elephant. Since elephants are unable to lie down for long before their weight impairs their breathing, the operation was performed with Win Thida anesthetized standing up, the veterinarian using a ladder to climb up and insert the lens.

60 EYES▶ A new species of flatworm that has a staggering 60 eyes in its body—but that is just 0.5 in (12 mm) long—has been found by scientists near Cambridge, England.

PET TIGER▶ Michael Jamison and Jackie Smit share their home in Brakpan, South Africa, with 14 dogs and a 378-lb (172-kg) Bengal tiger called Enzo, which they bought as a cub. He used to ride in their yellow Lamborghini until his daily diet of 11 lb (5 kg) of meat meant he grew too big.

BRAIN OVERSPILL ▶ Some tiny spiders measuring less than 0.04 in (1 mm) across have such a huge brain for their body size—taking up nearly 80 percent of their total body space— that their brain actually spills over into their legs.

▲ Photographers arrive to take shots of Eli as the local tiger sharks come to play with him.

▲ A tiger shark comes in for a "high-five" with Eli.

◀ Diver Eli Martinez has trained deadly, 16-ft-long (5-m) tiger sharks— second only to great whites in terms of attacking humans— to roll around like playful puppies just by tickling them. The shark whisperer, from Alamo, Texas, has been visiting Tiger Beach off the Bahamas for ten years and has struck up such a bond with the local sharks that he can get them to "high-five" him with their fins and even roll 360 degrees around his hand. He is still very cautious, though, and aware that "they are so wild you can never get 100 percent comfortable."

ALWAYS GROWING▶ Bowhead whales can live for more than 200 years, and because their spine does not fuse, they never stop growing.

READING SKILLS▶ Baboons can learn reading skills. In 300,000 tests conducted by French scientists, six baboons were able to distinguish between real and fake words flashed up on a computer screen 75 percent of the time. The star of the group, four-year-old Dan, achieved an 80-percent success rate and learned to recognize 308 four-letter words.

CRUSH-TACEANS▶ Florida stone crabs have crushing claws that can exert a force of up to 19,000 lb per square inch (1,336 kg/cm^2)—several times stronger than an industrial car crusher.

URINE WASH▶ Male capuchin monkeys make themselves more attractive to females by urinating onto their hands and then rubbing the urine into their fur like a human would rub cologne onto the skin. When a fertile female capuchin is on the hunt for a male partner, the smell of the male's urine indicates to her that he is sexually mature and available.

ELEPHANT DETERRENT▶ Farmers in Tanzania have devised a new way to keep elephants off their land—by smearing fences with a mixture of chili peppers and engine oil. The elephants never forget the intense burning smell of the chilis, which makes them sneeze, while the engine oil helps the spicy concoction stick to the fences, even in heavy rain.

MILK MACHINE▶ Smurf, a 15-year-old Holstein cow from Embrun, Canada, has produced over 57,000 gal (216,000 l) of milk in her lifetime—three times more than the average dairy cow and equal to more than one million glasses of milk.

CHIMP HANDSHAKES▶ Chimpanzees pass down a secret handshake through the generations—and the form of the handshake differs from group to group. Researchers in Zambia found that some chimps prefer to clasp hands while others like to clutch the wrists.

BEAR RIDE▶ In December 2011, a black bear made its way into downtown Vancouver, Canada, by hitching a ride in a garbage truck. The bear had been hunting for food in a dumpster when the dumpster's contents, including the bear, were tipped into the truck.

HIGH LIFE▶ When Richard Haughton goes to work repairing the thatched roofs of cottages in Norfolk, England, his dog Axel joins him up on the roof. Axel, a Labrador, Newfoundland, and Rottweiler cross, catches a lift on his owner's shoulder to get up and down the ladder and shows no fear of heights.

BEES' NEST▶ Tommy Hill of Brighton, Tennessee, found that 25,000 bees had made their home in the engine of his car overnight. He tried to lose them by driving down the highway at 60 mph (96 km/h), but not one bee left the nest until eventually they were all lured out with a box of honey.

WAXY MORSEL▶ In addition to feeding on the ticks and parasites of Africa's large mammals, red-billed oxpecker birds dine on the mammals' tears, saliva, mucus, blood, and earwax!

FAT CAT▶ Believed to be the world's fattest cat, Sponge Bob weighed 33 lb (15 kg)—the same as a four-year-old child—when he first arrived at an animal shelter in Manhattan, New York City.

FLYING CAT▶ Sugar the cat fell 19 stories from a high-rise window in Boston, Massachusetts, and walked away without any broken bones or cuts.

TRAPPED BULL▶ A bull fell through an open manhole in Santiago, Chile, and spent two days trapped in the drainage ditch before the animal was finally rescued.

PARROT DIALECTS▶ Since many of a parrot's calls are learned rather than instinctive, parrot populations often develop local dialects in their songs, depending on what birds they grew up with.

SPLIT PERSONALITY

▶*Venus, a chimera cat from North Carolina, has become a celebrity on Facebook because her face appears to be perfectly divided into two halves. Her face is half black and half calico, and the condition heterochromia has given her one blue eye and one green.*

PYTHON PASSENGER

▶ A 16-ft-long (5-m) python made its home under the hood of Marlene Swart and Leon Swanepoel's car while they were on holiday in South Africa's Kruger National Park. When the reptile refused to budge, they had to drive the stowaway snake 3 mi (4.8 km) to the nearest lookout point, where they were finally able to remove it.

TIGHTROPE WALKER▶ An Alaskan malamute dog in Chongqing, China, has learned to walk a tightrope and can walk along two parallel 33-ft-long (10-m) wires in just a minute. Wang Xianting and his colleagues have been training dogs so that they can access difficult areas and help firefighters deal with disasters.

GLOWING DONKEYS▶ 500 donkeys in Botswana were fitted with glow-in-the-dark ear tags in an attempt to reduce the number of accidents on country roads at night. The animals' impoverished owners often leave them to roam freely in search of food, and in northern Botswana one in ten road crashes involves a donkey.

MONSTER SNAKE▶ A female Burmese python caught in the Florida Everglades in 2012 measured 17.6 ft (5.3 m) long, weighed almost 165 lb (75 kg), and was carrying an incredible 87 eggs.

BRAVERY AWARD▶ Yogi the golden retriever won a heroic dog award for rescuing his owner in true Lassie style. When Paul Horton of Austin, Texas, was knocked unconscious after falling off his bicycle, Yogi ran to get help, finding Horton's neighbors and barking at them until they followed him back to the injured cyclist.

BALD HEDGEHOG

▶ Betty the hedgehog suffers from a mystery skin condition that has left her without any spines. Abandoned by her mother, Betty was taken to an animal rescue center in Norfolk, England, where she has to stay out of the sun because her skin is so dry and sensitive. The youngster is scared of other hedgehogs, which may make it impossible for her to find a mate.

LOT OF BULL▶ Jocko, a 27-year-old bull from France, died in March 2012 after fathering 400,000 offspring during his lifetime. By donating 1.7 million sperm straws, Jocko helped keep alive the Prim'Holstein cattle strain, and in France alone, his daughters are present in over 23,000 farms.

CAT COMMUTER▶ Graeme, a cat belonging to Nicole Weinrich of Melbourne, Australia, follows his owner to the train every day when she leaves for work—then returns to the station to wait for her at the end of the day. Occasionally, he even jumps on to the train and rides for a couple of stations before getting off again.

MUSICAL ELEPHANT▶ Shanthi, a 36-year-old Asian elephant at the Smithsonian National Zoo in Washington, D.C., has started playing the harmonica. She uses her trunk to play the instrument, which is attached to the side of her enclosure.

RAY ATTACK▶ Jenny Hausch was boating off the coast of Islamorada, Florida, when a 300-lb (136-kg) spotted eagle ray leapt from the water into her boat, pinning her to the deck.

HAPPY SNAP

▶ Photographer Marina Scarr captured this image of a hapless gar fish jumping straight into the jaws of a hungry alligator in Florida's Myakka River. The water level was low at the time and the fish did not stand much chance as there were at least 70 other alligators in the river.

SHARK FALL▶ A live, 2-ft-long (60-cm) leopard shark fell from the sky and landed near the 12th tee on San Juan Hills Golf Club in California. The shark had puncture wounds where it appeared that a bird had grabbed it from the Pacific Ocean some 5 mi (8 km) away. Club officials rushed the injured shark back to the ocean and it swam off.

TALKING ELEPHANT▶ A 22-year-old male Asian elephant called Koshik can mimic human speech and say five words in Korean—hello, no, sit down, lie down, and good. A resident of Everland Zoo in South Korea, Koshik puts the tip of his trunk into his mouth to transform his natural low rumble into a convincing impression of the human voice.

WRESTLED GATOR▶ Sixty-six-year-old grandfather Steve Gustafson from Lake County, Florida, wrestled a 7-ft-long (2.1-m), 130-lb (60-kg) alligator to pry his West Highland terrier Bounce from the reptile's jaws. Seeing the alligator heading into the water with the little dog in its mouth, Gustafson made a flying leap onto the creature's back and fought it underwater until he was able to free Bounce. When the gator snapped at his hand, he grabbed its jaw and pinned it shut. After swimming off, the alligator was killed by a trapper a few days later and bought by Gustafson to be stuffed as a permanent reminder of his crazy wrestling match.

CLEVER BOY!▶ A pet cockatoo named Figaro from Vienna, Austria, has learned to use his beak to make tools from sticks so that he can get at food that would otherwise be out of his reach. He is able to cut twigs to the right size to grab nuts placed outside his cage. Wild cockatoos are not known for making tools, and scientists believe Figaro is the first cockatoo to do so.

> **▶▶ A PLATYPUS CAN STORE 600 EARTHWORMS IN ITS CHEEK POUCHES FOR FOOD. ◀**

DOLPHIN ALERT▶ Dolphins can stay awake for at least 15 days by sleeping with only one half of their brain at a time. This allows them to remain alert and active so that they can regularly come to the surface to breathe and keep a constant lookout for predatory sharks.

SECURITY CAT▶ A major toy warehouse in Southampton, England, employed a cat as a security guard to protect its Christmas stock. Millie the Bengal cat secured the post through her excellent climbing abilities and loud purr. She was paid with cat food and fish.

CROC ESCAPE▶ Baggage handlers at Melbourne Airport, Australia, had a shock when they began unloading passengers' luggage from the hold of a Qantas airplane—and found a crocodile running loose. The reptile was being transferred from Brisbane but had escaped from its container during the two-hour flight.

DEADLY BITE▶ A single bite from the inland taipan or fierce snake of Australia contains enough venom to kill 100 adult men or 250,000 mice within 45 minutes. Yet because it rarely comes into contact with people, there are very few recorded human deaths from its bite.

TRUNK AND DISORDERLY▶ Fifty elephants went on a drunken rampage in Dumurkota, India, after drinking 18 containers of mahua, a strong alcoholic brew. The herd demolished dozens of houses, ransacked a shop, and ruined crops in their search for more liquor.

NEW TEETH▶ An Australian saltwater crocodile's teeth are constantly replaced. The toothy animals go through 3,000 teeth in a lifetime.

LOW TRICK▶ Zookeepers in Linyi, China, trained a giraffe to duck so that the animal could pass under more than 20 low bridges, electricity pylons, and highway signs on the journey to her new home. They spent months teaching 15-year-old Mengmeng to dip her head whenever she saw a low obstacle, but it still took seven hours to move her just a few miles.

PARALYSIS CURE▶ Paralyzed in an accident, Jasper the dachshund lost the use of his hind legs until scientists at Cambridge University, England, injected cells from the dog's nose into the injured part of his spine so that he could walk again.

SAVED LIFE▶ When Aysha Perry from Nottinghamshire, England, started choking on a piece of chicken, her Japanese Akita dog Sheba saved her life by bounding into the room and hitting her on the back with one of her huge paws, dislodging the piece of meat. Afterward, Sheba licked her owner's face to make sure she was okay.

BEAVER COLLECTION▶ Since starting her collection in the 1970s, Betty Davis of Redlands, California, has acquired more than 600 different items of beaver-related memorabilia.

DOGGY DRIVER

▶ A dog in New Zealand has been taught to drive a car. Having first put the car into gear, with his left front paw on the steering wheel and his right back foot on the accelerator (modified so that he could reach it), Porter steered a Mini Cooper along an off-road track in Auckland. Porter's two months of daily instruction by trainer Mark Vette began with mock car controls, then moved on to a real car with an instructor, until finally Porter performed his solo test. The Auckland Society for the Prevention of Cruelty to Animals wanted to showcase how clever dogs are.

SPIDER RIDER

▶ This close-up of a female wolf spider shows it carrying hundreds of young spiderlings on its back. The wolf spider is the only spider that carries her eggs in a round silken globe attached to her abdomen—much like a human would carry a growing baby. When the eggs hatch, they move on to the mother's back until they are old enough to hunt on their own.

ROLY POLY▶ A hedgehog at an animal rescue center in Somerset, England, was so fat that he was unable to roll into a ball. Roly Poly weighed 4 lb 7 oz (2 kg), more than three times the weight of an average hedgehog.

JOINED RACE▶ A stray dog ran for 1,138 mi (1,830 km) and 24 days to keep pace with a bicycle race across China. Xiao Sa's amazing journey began when one of the cyclists fed her, and she then joined the long-distance race from Wuhan to Llasa, in the process climbing ten mountains higher than 13,000 ft (4,000 m).

FOSTER MOM▶ After being rejected by her natural mother, a baby chimpanzee at a Russian zoo was adopted by the keeper's 100-lb (45-kg) pet mastiff dog. Within hours, the chimp had settled in and started eating and sleeping with the family's dogs.

FRISBEE CATCH▶ Sixty dogs from six countries demonstrated their Frisbee-catching skills at the 2012 Extreme Distance Frisbee European Championships for Dogs in Budapest, Hungary. Categories include toss and fetch and freestyle, where the dogs perform a routine to music.

SURFING GOAT▶ Wearing her yellow life jacket, "Goatee" the goat regularly surprises beachcombers on California's Pismo Beach by balancing her hooves on the surfboard of her owner Dana McGregor, and riding the waves.

EMERGENCY CALL▶ George, a two-year-old basset hound, saved his own life in March 2012 by dialing emergency services after becoming strangled by the cord of an old-fashioned phone. George had knocked over the heavy phone in owner Steve Brown's home in West Yorkshire, England, but despite choking with the cord wrapped around his neck, managed to dial 999 with his paw. The emergency operator heard heavy breathing and gasping on the other end of the line and alerted medics and a neighbor.

DOGGIE WHEELS▶ Eighteen months after breaking her back, Carnage, a shih tzu-Maltese cross, can run around again thanks to a set of $300 wheels. Owner Jude McMinn from Queensland, Australia, bought the wheels, which replace the dog's back legs, after being told Carnage would have to be put down.

RARE KITTEN▶ At the Audubon Center for Research of Endangered Species in New Orleans, an ordinary domestic cat has been used as a surrogate mother to create a rare African black-footed kitten. In a world first, nine-year-old frozen sperm from African black-footed cats, of which there are fewer than 10,000 left in the wild, was used to form embryos that were transplanted by IVF into the house cat.

Believe It or Not!®
www.ripleybooks.com

POOP SNIFFER ▶ A black Labrador mix named Tucker has been trained to become the only working dog able to sniff out and track the scent of killer whale feces in the ocean as far as a mile away. By detecting the orca scat around the San Juan Islands, Washington State, the one-time Seattle stray helps marine biologists monitor the health of the whales.

FRIEND OF THE STARS ▶ In his lifetime, Lucky, a little white Maltese dog owned by U.S. TV personality and animal campaigner Wendy Diamond, was photographed with more than 300 famous people, including ex-President Bill Clinton, TV personality Kim Kardashian, movie star Kristen Stewart, and musician Kanye West. Sadly, Lucky died in June 2012 at age 15 from spleen cancer.

PERMA-KITTEN ▶ Lil Bub, a dwarf cat from Bloomington, Indiana, is a perma-kitten, meaning that she will be the size of a kitten and have kittenlike features for her entire life. She was born with several genetic mutations, making her legs disproportionately small compared with the rest of her body. She has no teeth but has an extra toe on each foot, giving her a total of 22 claws—four more than is usual.

DUCK DRIVE

▶ *A farmer holds up traffic while driving a huge herd of 5,000 ducks along a road on their way to a pond in Taizhou, China. Farmer Hong has been herding his ducks through the city for several months and claims never to have lost a single one.*

MONKEY BUSINESS ▶ A white-capped capuchin monkey has become such a talented artist that 40 of his paintings were exhibited in Toronto, Canada, in 2011. Pockets Warhol, a resident of Story Book Farm, a primate sanctuary in Sunderland, Ontario, paints with his tail, hands, feet, and sometimes a brush. His colorful artworks have been sold for up to $400 apiece to buyers from as far afield as Europe and Israel.

DOUBLE TROUBLE

▶ A pig in Zhangjia, China, was born with two mouths—and it eats and drinks through both of them. The strange little piggy also has two snouts. These deformities prevented it from suckling, so farmer Bai Xuejin fed it by hand until it was old enough to take solid food.

ILLUMINATED CREATURES

Female glowworm

▶ Adult **female glowworms** use the eerie green light at the base of their abdomen to attract mates. Once a female has mated, she turns out her light, lays her eggs, and dies.

▶ Living in the depths of the Atlantic, where there is no light, the female **anglerfish** entices prey with a fishing-rod-like projection from its mouth, the end of the rod being illuminated by bacteria.

▶ The **hatchetfish** emits greenish-white lights as a defensive camouflage. When sunlight on the water casts a shadow of the fish, it turns on its lights to disguise the shadow and hide from predators below.

▶ The **cookiecutter shark** glows luminescent green for camouflage, but a small patch on its underbelly remains dark so that it resembles a small fish to hungry tuna and mackerel, which are then eaten by the shark when they attack.

▶ A species of **giant South American cockroach** has three glowing spots on its back to mimic the appearance of the toxic click beetle, thereby deterring predators.

▶ **Headlight beetles** of the West Indies emit so much light that islanders used to tie a few to their toes so they could see where they were going at night.

FAMOUS PEOPLE AND THEIR PETS

▶ Nineteenth-century English nurse **Florence Nightingale** rescued a **baby owl** when she visited Athens, smuggled it home, and often kept it in her pocket.

▶ As a boy, Aerosmith front man **Steven Tyler** had a **raccoon** that he used to take on fishing trips.

▶ French poet **Gérard de Nerval** used to walk his **lobster** on a length of ribbon through Parisian gardens.

▶ Spanish painter **Salvador Dalí** owned an **ocelot**, Babou, which traveled everywhere with him, even on luxury cruise liners.

▶ Sixteenth-century Danish astronomer **Tycho Brahe** had a **moose** that used to roam free during parties and drink large amounts of alcohol.

▶ English poet **Lord Byron** kept a **bear** at Cambridge University—because dogs were not allowed.

▶ **Michael Jackson's chimpanzee** Bubbles slept in a crib in the singer's room and even used his toilet.

▶ U.S. President **John Quincy Adams** had an **alligator**—a gift from the Marquis de Lafayette—which he used to keep in a bathroom in the White House.

▶ **Napoleon Bonaparte's wife Josephine** had an **orangutan** that was allowed to join her at the table for meals.

ANIMAL CANNIBALS

Tamarin monkeys

▶ The female Australian **redback spider** often devours the smaller male during mating.

▶ While still in the womb, **baby sand tiger sharks** develop teeth, which they use to eat their younger siblings. The mother has two uteruses and only one pup survives in each of them.

▶ A **Papuan python** was once found with a carpet python in its stomach.

▶ **Mormon crickets** walk up to 50 mi (80 km) in a migratory season in search of food—and if one cricket stops marching, the others will eat it.

▶ Less than 1 percent of **freshwater crocodile** eggs grow into adults—with cannibalism one of the major causes of mortality in young crocs.

▶ **Spotted hyena cubs** practice their hunting skills on their brothers and sisters, mauling them to death even as the adults try to separate them.

▶ **Female green anacondas** that can grow 16 ft (5 m) long and weigh 215 lb (97.5 kg) sometimes eat their smaller male partners in order to survive their seven months of pregnancy.

▶ A hungry **female praying mantis** often bites off the male's head while mating, but his sex drive is so strong that he can continue to mate even while being slowly eaten.

▶ Although they are usually devoted mothers, **tamarin monkeys** have also been seen biting

ANIMALS
THAT SAVED HUMANS

▶ When a rattlesnake attacked 11-year-old Sean Callahan in Texas, Leo, a poodle, leaped between the snake and the boy. Despite receiving six potentially deadly bites to the head, Leo survived, and saved Sean from the attack.

▶ Seeing surfer Adam Maguire attacked by a shark near Sydney, Australia, a school of dolphins thrashed around in the water, circled the shark repeatedly, and chased it to stop it moving in for the kill.

▶ Schnautzie the kitten alerted Trudy Guy to a potentially fatal gas leak at her Montana home by repeatedly tapping her on the nose and sniffing the air.

▶ Priscilla, a pig owned by Victoria Herberta of Houston, Texas, rescued 11-year-old Anthony Melton from drowning in Somerville Lake by swimming to his aid, using her snout to keep his head above water until he could hold on to her collar, and then dragging him to the shore.

▶ After Noel Osborne shattered his hip in a fall at his farm in Benalla, Australia, his goat Mandy huddled by his side for five cold days and nights, not only keeping him warm but also allowing him to milk her for sustenance.

▶ As a cougar prepared to pounce on 11-year-old Austin Forman in British Columbia, Canada, the boy's golden retriever Angel jumped directly into the big cat's path and bore the brunt of the attack instead.

▶ When a three-year-old boy fell into the gorilla enclosure at Brookfield Zoo, Illinois, Binti Jua, a female gorilla, guarded the boy from the other gorillas, then cradled him in her arms while her own baby was on her back and carried him to an entrance where keepers were able to retrieve him.

Fangtooth fish

FREAKY FISH

▶ The **globefish can inflate itself** to three times its normal size by filling an air bladder inside its body.

▶ The **climbing perch** uses its spiny gills and its fins to help it **climb trees.**

▶ Some species of **shark never stop swimming** even when they are asleep—if they did, they would drown.

▶ The **archerfish** squirts water up a tube between its tongue and palate to fire at insects sitting on leaves up to 3 ft (1 m) above the surface. The shot **knocks the insect off the leaf** and into the water where the fish is waiting to eat it.

▶ The **copperband butterflyfish** has a **false eye** near its tail so that enemies will think its tail is its head and therefore snap at the wrong end of the fish.

▶ The **swordfish** has a **special heater in its brain and eye muscles,** which keeps its vision sharp enough to catch food in dark depths of 2,000 ft (600 m).

▶ The **fangtooth** has the **largest teeth of any ocean fish,** proportionate to body size—about one-tenth of its total body length, the equivalent of adult humans having 10-in-long (25-cm) teeth.

FREQUENT FLYER ▶▶▶▶▶▶▶▶

Oscar the dog has visited more than 30 countries in three years, flying twice the circumference of the Earth and taking in such landmarks as the Great Wall of China, the Eiffel Tower in France, and the Golden Gate Bridge in California.

As well as traveling by airplane, he has also been up in a hot-air balloon and taken a helicopter ride over the Grand Canyon. He travels with owner Joanne Lefson, who rescued him from a South African kennel in 2004—just a day before he was due to be put down.

In India

At the Golden Gate Bridge

On board an airplane

Looking down on the Grand Canyon

At the Eiffel Tower

Vedettes du Pont Neuf

EN COMFORT▶ A male long-tailed macaque monkey in Bali's Ubud Monkey Forest adopted a stray ginger kitten, nuzzling and grooming it and caring for it as a pet.

SHRINKING HORSES▶ Early horses shrunk in size as the climate became warmer. When horses evolved around 56 million years ago, they were about the size of a small dog, but then became even smaller during a period of global warming. Then when the Earth's temperature subsequently cooled, horses dramatically increased in size.

RECORD TONGUE

▶ *Although he is only a fraction of the size of a Saint Bernard or a Great Dane, Puggy the Pekingese has got the opposition licked. For he is the dog with the world's longest tongue—a whopping 4½ in (11.43 cm). It is so long that it almost reaches the ground. He lives in Fort Worth, Texas, with owner Becky Stanford after having been abandoned as a puppy—perhaps because his oversize tongue made him look expensive to feed!*

BEAR NECESSITY▶ Two-year-old Lieke Stenbreker helped save the life of a baby sloth at a zoo in Arnhem, the Netherlands, by giving it her favorite teddy bear. The sloth's mother was not producing enough milk, so zookeepers tried feeding the baby by hand. However, attempts failed because baby sloths need to cuddle while they feed. Once Lieke had donated her teddy, the tiny sloth was able to cuddle the toy while taking milk from a syringe.

MUD RESCUE▶ Up to her waist in quicksand-like mud, Nicole Graham stayed by the side of her horse Astro for three hours, desperately keeping his head above water after the 1,100-lb (500-kg) animal had been swallowed up by the coastal mud near Geelong, Victoria, Australia. Astro was eventually pulled free by a farmer's tractor just minutes before the tide came in.

NUTS ABOUT MUSIC▶ Sammy, a gray squirrel adopted by piano teacher Shirley Higton of Yorkshire, England, has started playing his own miniature toy piano. After developing an interest during the Higton children's piano lessons, Sammy has learned to press the keys with his paws.

TRIPOD THE DUCK

▶ Ripley's were sent this picture of Tripod, a three-legged duck, by Robert Brooks from Concord, North Carolina. He says the three-legged duckling hatched on April 24, 2011, and despite the extra limb is perfectly healthy and well balanced.

ILLUMINATED WEBS▶ Orb weaver spiders spin webs that reflect ultraviolet light, making them visible to birds that would otherwise fly through the webs and ruin them.

LIVING PROOF▶ Until January 2012, when pictures were taken in remote mountain rain forests on the Burma–China border, the rare Myanmar snub-nosed monkey—*Rhinopithecus strykeri*—had never been photographed alive. Before that, the species had been described only from a dead specimen collected by a local hunter.

HEAVY PATIENT▶ When a 1,050-lb (477-kg) polar bear at the Highland Wildlife Park in Inverness-shire, Scotland, developed a toothache, it needed 12 dentists, veterinarians, and dental nurses to carry out a three-hour root canal operation. The dentist's chair for five-year-old Arktos consisted of a specially reinforced table made from scaffolding poles and planks.

GOAT TOWER▶ The Fairview Farm in Paarl, South Africa, has a two-story tower built for the exclusive use of the farm's 750 goats. The tower was built with spiral staircases as goats can climb more efficiently when the object they are climbing is positioned at an angle.

ELEPHANT MAN▶ Known locally as "the Elephant Man," Andy Swan of Sacramento, California, has collected more than 10,000 elephant-related items, including miniature models, plush toys, jewelry, album covers, and clothing.

TWO-HEADED BIRD ▶ Hearing a commotion in the backyard of her home in Northampton, Massachusetts, April Britt went out to investigate and found a baby Cardinal chick with two heads and three beaks.

TWO-LEGGED KITTEN ▶ A video showing a two-legged kitten playing with a ball and a feather went viral on YouTube. Found and adopted by artist Carrie Hawks from Pensacola, Florida, little Anakin was born without a pelvis and his two back legs. He manages to get around by pushing his front feet back, so that they are almost in the middle of his body, and using his tail for balance.

SNOWBOARDING OPOSSUM

▶ Ratatouille, a snowboarding opossum, has become such a celebrity at the Liberty Mountain Resort in Pennsylvania that he even has his own lift pass. Wearing his favorite green sweater, he regularly takes to the slopes atop a special mini snowboard that he steers with the help of his tail.

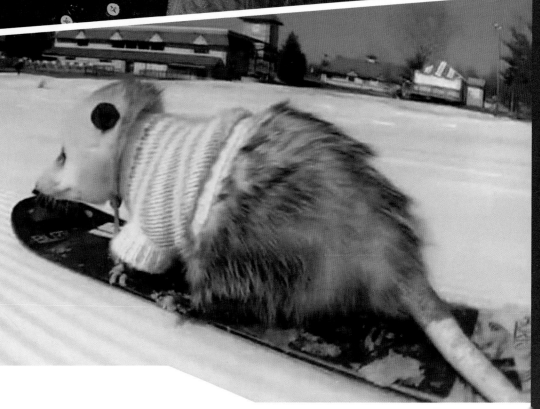

MUMMIFIED PETS

Dozens of pet owners have chosen to have their favorite pets mummified after death, preserving their corpses in animal-shaped caskets to keep them as fresh as the day they died. The bodies of beloved cats, dogs, rats, finches, and even peacocks have been sent to the world's only pet mummification company to undergo the traditional burial routine of the Ancient Egyptians.

When a client's pet dies, the vet packs the body in ice and transports it to the Salt Lake City, Utah, headquarters of Summum, whose office building is, appropriately, pyramid-shaped. The pet's organs are removed and cleansed before being placed back inside the body. The corpse is then hydrated by submerging it in a water tank for at least 70 days. The Egyptians preferred to dehydrate bodies, but Summum finds that they are better preserved by doing the opposite. The dead pet is then smeared with lanolin and wax, wrapped in bandages, and given a fiberglass finish.

▲ *A number of humans have also signed up to be mummified—one of the benefits of the process being the fact that it could soon be possible to remove a person's DNA for cloning after death by drilling into the casket. Ron Temu, a client counselor at Summum, says: "Being able to take out DNA at a later date has real appeal for people. They like the idea of being able to clone themselves."*

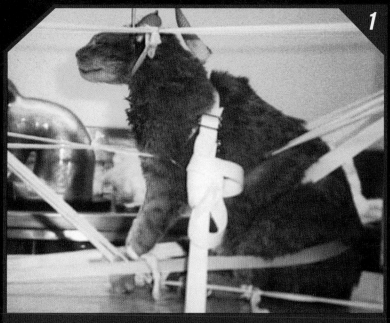

1

▲ After its organs are removed, cleaned, and put back inside the body, the hydrated dead cat is suspended in position ready to be wrapped in bandages.

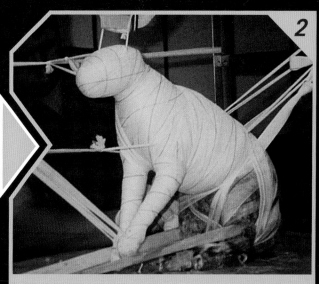

2

▲ The body is swathed in several layers of cotton gauze in keeping with Egyptian mummification tradition.

5

▶ Finally the pet is encased in a casket, ranging from standard bronze to ornate gold with jewels. The whole process can take up to ten months and costs from $7,000 for a cat to over $80,000 for a Great Dane. The company will even mummify horses.

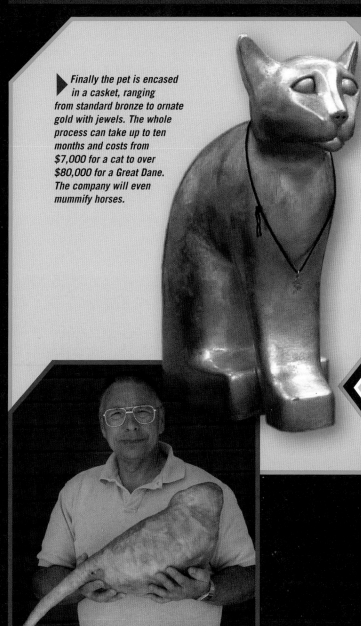

▲ A mummified peacock.

3

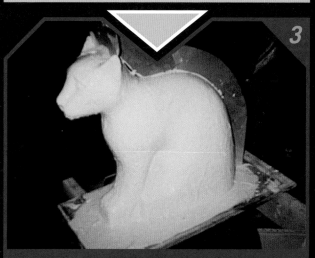

▲ A polyurethane membrane is then coated over the gauze to form a permanent seal before adding a layer of fiberglass and resin.

4

▲ Pet caskets or mummiforms come in bronze, marble, and, in this case, exotic gold leaf that is applied with a range of brushes.

SPOT THE DIFFERENCE▶ Zoe, a Dalmatian dog at a farm in South Australia's Barossa Valley, adopted a look-alike lamb, which had a black-and-white spotty coat. The lamb was so confused by the resemblance that he even tried to suckle from the dog, who responded by allowing him to sleep inside her kennel.

DOG DOCTOR▶ Sharon Rawlinson from Nottinghamshire, England, discovered she had a cancerous tumor in her breast only because Penny, her Cavalier King Charles Spaniel, kept sniffing and pawing at it. The dog's bizarre behavior continued for several months until finally Penny stepped on her owner's chest, causing sufficient pain to trigger Sharon into investigating further. Closer inspection revealed the lump.

WEALTHY KITTY▶ In 2011, Tommaso, a lucky black cat who was rescued from the streets of Rome, Italy, and given a home by an elderly widowed heiress, inherited nearly $13 million from her in the form of cash, shares, and a property empire including homes in Rome and Milan and land in Calabria. Maria Assunta had become so enamored with her adopted pet that, two years before her death, she wrote out a will bequeathing her entire estate to Tommaso.

INK CLOUDS▶ Caribbean reef squid hide from predators by squirting out clouds of ink and then disguising themselves to look like the billows of ink that they just created.

PORCUPINE ATTACK

▶ When bulldog Bella Mae got into a fight with a porcupine near her home in Norman, Oklahoma, she ended up with 500 quills stuck in her face, neck, legs, chest, and paws—though miraculously they all missed her eyes. Porcupines hit victims with their tail, leaving some of their 30,000 barbed quills embedded in the skin. Veterinarians eventually managed to dig out the quills and set Bella Mae on the road to recovery.

BLIND FISH▶ Mexico's blind cave fish are actually born with eyes, but skin soon grows over them and they are rendered sightless. They find their way around by bouncing sound waves off nearby objects.

LONG JOURNEY▶ A calico cat named Willow that belonged to the Squires family of Boulder, Colorado, and went missing in 2006, was found five years later roaming the streets of Manhattan, more than 1,800 mi (2,900 km) away.

GUARDIAN ANGEL▶ One night, Patricia Peter from Camrose, Canada, was woken by her cat Monty repeatedly biting the fingers of her left hand—the hand she used to monitor her blood-sugar levels for her recently diagnosed diabetes. When she woke, Patricia felt sick, whereupon Monty ran and sat beside her diabetic testing kit. Taking her cue from the cat, Patricia discovered that, sure enough, her blood-sugar levels were dangerously low. Monty persisted in keeping Patricia awake until they returned to normal.

FIVE LEGS▶ Benny, a five-year-old dog owned by Leah Garcia of Texas, has five legs, with an extra limb located under his right front paw. He has three elbows and five paws but walks on only three legs, as his two right front legs are nonfunctional. Leah adopted Benny after he was abandoned at her workplace as a puppy.

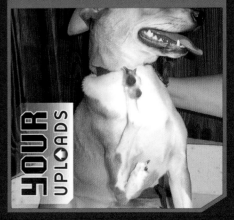

YOUR UPLOADS

FEEDING FRENZY

> Although they weigh up to 79,000 lb (36,000 kg) and measure as much as 52 ft (16 m) long, humpback whales regularly lift 90 percent of their body out of the water before twisting and landing on their back—an action known as breaching. Attracted by a mass of sardines, this hungry humpback surfaced in shallow waters near San Luis Obispo, California, to the amazement of kayakers and sailors who were able to get within a few feet of the ocean giant. The picture was taken by Bill Bouton, who had been trying unsuccessfully to photograph birds until his luck changed with a picture that got 200,000 views within 16 hours of being posted on Flickr.

GROUNDHOG DAY▶ In the period around Independence Day 2012, groundhogs removed more than 75 flags from Civil War graves in Cedar Park Cemetery, Hudson, New York. Police identified the culprits after special cameras revealed a number of flags hidden down the animals' underground holes.

LAST STRAW▶ Crunchie, a male strawberry roan Welsh mountain pony, has to sleep on a bed of shredded waste paper at his stable in Cheshire, England, because he suffers from hay fever! He was diagnosed as being allergic to the dust in traditional straw beds after suffering a near-fatal asthma attack in 2009.

TWO HEADS▶ A two-headed California kingsnake was born at a zoo in Yalta, Ukraine. The snake's two heads eat separately and react differently, so one head has to be isolated with a special spatula to prevent the second head from blocking its swallowing.

PURPLE COW▶ In January 2012, a black-and-white cow in Cacak, Serbia, gave birth to a calf with purple-tinted fur. The coloring is thought by doctors to be some kind of genetic mutation.

SPEED KINGS▶ Houston Zoo, Texas, has borrowed a racetrack so that its pair of five-year-old cheetah brothers, Kito and Kiburi, can stretch their legs. Adult cheetahs need a 200-yd (182-m) straight run for healthy exercise, and with space limited at the zoo, they were able to approach their top speed of 65 mph (104 km/h) at the nearby Sam Houston Race Park.

STOWAWAY CAT▶ A stowaway black-and-white cat survived with just minor burns after riding 200 mi (320 km) through Ohio, from Xenia to Cleveland, under the hood of a car.

PIG RECRUIT▶ A 200-lb (91-kg) pig called Dominic has joined Avon Fire and Rescue Service in England to help firefighters learn how to handle escaped animals.

ROUND TRIP▶ The northern wheatear, a tiny 1-oz (28-g) songbird, makes an epic, annual 18,600-mi (29,930-km) round-trip migratory journey between sub-Saharan Africa and the bird's Arctic breeding grounds.

DOLPHIN CALLS▶ Although each dolphin has its own individual whistle, dolphins often communicate by mimicking the sounds of their closest companions. Research shows that the mammals' signature whistles copy only those dolphins they share strong social bonds with and want to be reunited with.

SLAM DUNK▶ Eddie, a 16-year-old sea otter at The Oregon Zoo in Portland, Oregon, has started playing basketball in his pool to help ease his arthritis. To the delight of visitors, he picks up a plastic ball, swims with it toward a specially built, low-level hoop, and then slam dunks it in the basket.

INDEX

ACKNOWLEDGMENTS

Cover (r) Liberty Mountain Resort, (l) Caters News/worldwooftour.com; **4** Kyndra Batla; **6** (t) Reuters/Cris Toala Olivares, (b) Matt Roper; **7** (c) Matt Roper, (b) Reuters/Fred Thornhill;
8 (t) © Pete Oxford/NaturePL.com, (b) Charles Lam/Rex Features; **9** (t) Caters News, (b) Reuters/Chaiwat Subprasom; **10** (b/l) ZSSD/Minden Pictures/FLPA, (b/r) Michael Patricia
Fogden/Minden Pictures/National Geographic Stock; **11** University of California at Davis Veterinary School; **12** (t) Europics, (b) Caters News; **13** Caters News; **14** (t) Imagine China,
(b) Martin Amm; **15** Kyndra Batla; **16–17** Caters News; **18** NBCU Photo Bank via Getty Images; **19** (t) Caters News, (b) Albanpix Ltd/Rex Features; **20** Caters News; **21** (t) Draft FCB
New Zealand/SPCA, (b) © Bruce Coleman/Photoshot; **22–23** (t) Imagine China; **23** (b) Europics; **24** (t) © NHPA/Photoshot, (b) © Eric Gevaert - Fotolia.com;
25 © David Shale/NaturePL.com; **26–27** Caters News/worldwooftour.com; **28** (b) Becky Stanford, (t) Robert Brooks; **29** Liberty Mountain Resort; **30–31** Worldwide Features;
32 (l) Sipa USA/Rex Features, (r) Leah Garcia; **33** Photo by Bill Bouton; **Back cover** Kyndra Batla

Key: t = top, b = bottom, c = center, l = left, r = right, sp = single page, dp = double page

All other photos are from Ripley Entertainment Inc.
Every attempt has been made to acknowledge correctly and contact copyright holders and we apologize in advance
for any unintentional errors or omissions, which will be corrected in future editions.